BELOW THE
MAYONNAISE FACTORY

POEMS

Earl LeClaire

Second Edition

Earl LeClaire

Original title
BELOW THE MAYONNAISE FACTORY

Cover image
Earl LeClaire

Layout
Yossi Faybish
Sonja Smolec

Published by
Aquillrelle

Printed in the United States of America, Second Edition.

ISBN 978-1-329-35863-8

Table of Contents

THE MIRROR'S THIN EDGE

Some of these poems have appeared in the following magazines and anthologies: *Panurge: Magazine of New Writing* (UK), *Southern Illinois University Press, Sou'Wester* (US), *Great Swamp Gazette* (US), *Frank* (F), *Praguenosis* (CZ), *A Letter Among Friends* (US), *Brown University Press, Literary Fruit* (US), *Earth Day News* (US), *Russian River Anthology* (US), *TomCat: Showcase of Northern California Poets* (US), *University of California at Davis: Carver Magazine* (US), *HolyBoyRoad. Com* (US).

BELOW THE
MAYONNAISE FACTORY

Tattered Flags

"Isn't this your life? That ancient kiss
still burning out your eyes? Isn't this defeat
so accurate, the church bell simply seems
a pure announcement: ring and no one comes?
Don't empty houses ring?"

~Richard Hugo

Below the Mayonnaise Factory

Below the mayonnaise factory
Where my mother worked,
The hills dropped
Heavy hearts to streets
That cut their way
To the river that lay
A dead and rotting snake.

Mean streets that sliced
Through tenement houses
Where tattered flags of wash
Hung from every window
And angry mothers shouted
From open doorways
For their fugitive sons.
Down through to the maiming mills
That squatted like fat,
Panatela smoking bosses
On the rivers black banks.

No quaint cobblestone there,
Prehistoric tar,
Murderous asphalt,
Crowded and cluttered
With junked cars and trash
And the abandoned bodies of wet winos,
My precious clowns,
Who pissed their pants in the alleys
And whimpered like beaten puppies
Over a broken bottle of Tokay,
Losing that last poor pint of dignity,

Licking the glass and dirt and spilled wine,
Lapping that dread of life
That cripples as quick as polio
Off the polluted river.

Unholy streets
Packed with hoods and hung-over heroes:
Batman, Bundog, and Bennie-the-Book.
Heavy hitters with million-dollar dreams
And nickel brains,
Who thought with their fists
And loved with their cocks.
Fathers, uncles and older sons,
Their misplaced manhood a sham, a charlatan
A sucker-punch delivered by a green-toothed whore.
And now, years later, writing this poem,
They are with me again, as they have always been
My constant shadow, my drunk-day self,
My fearsome other, those streets,
Etched into my being as permanent
As the scars carved into my skin.

The Garden

Behind the window
That viewed the garden,
That was our window
From the other side,
Old Lady Turisi sat
In a straight backed chair,
Aging with each garden grown,
Until there was only a shrivel
Behind the window,
A shrivel clinging to her cane
Like a withered apple
Stemmed to the branch in December;
A shrivel framed by the casement
Like a Wyethian dream
Not yet to canvas.

What was there in that garden she guarded
That made her rap the glass with her cane
Or raise an arthritic fist in protest
When the other boys and I stole
A tomato or a handful of peas?
Crack, the cane would crack,
And a gnarled old fist come up,
And we would leap cannonballs
Over the New England wall,
Fall,
And stumble to the safety of thick-leaved trees
That wrapped the far side of the garden

And hid us from her old-woman-eyes,
Devil-hearted boys delighting in the garden game.

And on Novena nights
When all the other women in the village
Made their pilgrimage to the Immaculate Conception,
She alone remained, at the window,
Madonna of the Garden,
Mother of parsley and basil,
Guardian Saint of garlic and zucchini,
Watching in horror as her divined children
Were delivered into the harried hands
Of Satan-hearted boys.

And on, endless as they appeared,
The seasons of gardens, boys and old ladies sped
Until that night when, from behind the window
A woeful wailing filled the moon-borne garden
And sent blood rushing through bad-boy veins
And boy bodies hurtling for the safety of earth
Where, there, from our side,
We viewed black-shrouded women,
Old women,
Women older than all the ages of this planet,
Seated in straight back chairs,
Clinging to black bean beads,
Rising up, slowly up, with the moon
On the wailing's pitch.

Old Lady Turisi was dead.
And the days that followed came and went.

Wet, lifeless days that watched weeds grow,
That saw onion and broccoli pass to seed.
Gray, clouded days that found bad-blood boys
Standing behind the drizzle,
Under rain-laden trees,
Staring across the garden
To the horizon behind and empty window.

Explaining My Punk Past

The boy we called Sally Rags
Killed the alarm
Just as Bundog pried open the window.
The beer-joint was all ours.

Inside,
Rags and Bundog took the bar,
Manny and I took the machines.
The small change was all ours.

Someone dropped a crowbar
As it was our signal
To break bottles and smash mirrors.
The joy was all ours.

And we did it night after night,
Joint after joint,
Again and again.
And then they caught us.

And that's the part
I still feel bad about.

Little Leaguer Struck by Lightning Lives

It came like white dawn,
a light out of nowhere,
through the wall,
shooting studs and plaster
across the room,
twisting wire like burned strands of hair,
hurling him through the air,
slamming him face-first into the stove.

His head filled with celestial, circling,
blazing white, neon light;
quicksilver images that glittered and glistened
like newly minted coins in some gambling God's palm.

He was a kid again,
a Little Leaguer,
beaned by a high and wild fastball
thrown by a kid
twice his size.

He walked around for days,
guiding by stars,
gliding from New Moon to Mercury,
Mercury to Mars.
The voices he heard were mere mumbles
under the thunder of royal music and cannonade
from the Imperial Blast.

He realized his teeth had cracked
when their silver plugs
fell into his mouth.

He parted his lips to speak
and the hole glowed
like the molten heart of an ancient planet.
His eyes were headlamps with halogen centers
and flashing in the halo of his mind,
the result of some neural short-circuiting,
a vision of sparks and cinders
rising to ride the wind
like roman candles on the Fourth of July.

He went on like this day after day:
hearing the thunder,
staring into the sun,
smelling the charred orchards
of his arms and eyelashes.
All else became adjunct to the stream of pure light.

He took it as a sign of sanctification,
began to think of himself as the last sunrise
at the edge of the world.
Regarded it a blessing.
But, gradually, the light began to fade,
the vision became vapor-trail and small cloud,
the sound of thunder but a far and distant drum,
the smell turned to honeysuckle and sweat.

He panicked:
became more vigilant,
spent his nights and days watching for weather,
hoping for storm,
praying for volcanic dust to carry the charge.
For he knew that he was in danger
of becoming ordinary again.

Daddy Love and the Children of Divorce

I can write now
About that dead-ox-sun morning
When the cold Dorothy,
The wicked wizard cloud,
The unavoidable cyclone,
Rode in from the west on a shinplaster, shrouded wind.

I can tell you now, my daughters,
About that storm-bound time when your mother,
That bitter, blonde pearl,
Packed you into the Vega wagon with your cactus
Plant memories and Cleopatra cat
To run from the ruins of your parents' undoing.

How fragile you seemed under that cloud,
Tiny sprouts of spring wheat, sad stalks with tears
And small hands, clinging to your daddy.
Young wands of wheat waving goodbye
Through the spinning windmill wheels of your ten-speeds
Racked to the back. Goodbyes flickering
Silent movie flick-like
Through our unreasoning singular goodbye.
But how were we to reason anything
Under the shadow of that galena-colored cloud,
Slowly circling, gaining the weight of my despair?

You were leaving. Oh my children,
You were moving, sliding out from under.
And I knew, knowing all the while, knowing,
That the sounds of the road
And the accelerating landscape
Would blow away the dust of your tears
And roll them back to Denver
To gather like dry stones at my feet.

So I called on my wizardry
To send me hurling, Pecos Daddy Bill cloud
Through the prairie air, to cut you off at the pass,
And there to sweep you up and spin you home,
Home with your straw, balding mane, tin-mouthed Daddy.
I watched you cross into Kansas,
Into the land of spring wheat,
My young ones, my own, my munchkins,
Flickers of green slipping through the standing sheaves,
Sailing into the golden weed-grown, grain sca.
And I wondered then if Dorothy ever returned from Oz
Or just wished so hard for home
That the dream became reality.

The washed-out weathermen were
beset, beside themselves.
Where from this storm?
Your mother knew: as she kept the matrix of her turquoise eyes
On the rear-view, daddy-viewed mirror,
As Kansas traffic ducked into Stuckys'

And Nickerson Farms' and the jayhawkers
Into their rotting, root cellars
Holding their tunnel ears against the wailing,
Wind-filled, funnel, daddy-cloud crying your names.

And your mother, that nacreous concretion of shifting hues,
Hiding you, the nectar of my life in a roadside apiary,
Damning me, the wind-cloud wizard,
In my fruitless plains search
From Limon to Lawrence and back, slowly back,
The fury of my lead-ladened cloud, no-use misery lies
Blown to dust in a sad sigh.

As the spent wind-cloud wizard, bent,
To the will of a woman, the law's will,
Will of my own gander, peacock pride.
Your daddy, your shattered, heart-sinking
Life sunk daddy, I
Swept up the dust and put it in my pocket,
Locking it away until the day
I would roll it with the clay of the present
And use it, galena, crystal, tear-dust,
For the writing of this poem
As I continue to be, - Daddy Love.

The Woman with the Unpunched Ticket

The woman with the unpunched ticket
Stands solitary,
At the station,
With heavy baggage, waiting...
The woman with the unpunched ticket
Stands solitary,
At the station,
With heavy baggage, waiting,
Getting so
Damned
Im-
Patient...
The woman with the unpunched ticket stands
Solitary,
At the station,
With heavy baggage, waiting,
Getting so damned impatient for love...
The woman with the unpunched ticket
Stands solitary,
At the station,
With heavy baggage,
Waiting,
Getting so damned impatient for love
Like a passenger train,
Like a passenger train,
Like a passenger train
To come rolling
Clickity-clack,
Down the rails,
Covering ground
Like Amtrack times two.

The woman with the unpunched ticket,
The woman with the unpunched ticket,
She's waiting for love,
Waiting for love,
Waiting for love.

Note from Nepal

for Greg Mortenson and Susan Calamai

These are dangerous days,
Men with guns
Gather in close fields,
New hawks fly
Where no hawks have flown,
And the sun may well become
Something closer to earth.
Yet,
These are the very days
We need remember
That light enters
Even a boarded window,
Bends, and sweeps around the room,
A bright, warm river.
And that we also live
In that space between heartbeats,
Where the formless center
Of all things,
Is everywhere,
At once,
And forever.

In the Rain Dream

In the rain dream
the woman is Saint and Soul,
hears the moon
pulling tides,
knows it is she
who makes things grow.

Mud-caked men,
following old trails,
enter the dream.

The woman says,
"If you are lost,
let me find you."
The men, who have no
sense of direction,
refuse to admit it.

The woman says,
"If you are homeless,
let me offer shelter."
The men, who have forgotten
how to build homes
fill their mouths with nails.

The woman,
knowing the fierceness
of the men,
fills tubs with her tears,
offers baths.
The men refuse.

Finally
the woman says,
"I cannot do more for you than this.
Either bathe yourselves
or drown."

The Creation Dream

In the masque
of the creation dream
female moon is diamond,
facets infinite.

A ram stands on the distant horizon.
What is close is felt, not described.

Listen to women...

The cock crows itself to sleep.
The bird sings itself awake.

It is the woman who makes things grow.

The woman unfolds her apron,
shakes out children
as if they are seeds,
as if they are stars.

Listen to women...

Aftermath

after George Hubert Bush and Saddam Hussein

For days
the child lay
without a grave
beside the river.

How shall the dark wine be drunk,
the dead child known?

The entire week was one long wailing.
Those who said, Praise God,
knelt down in ruins
while mothers and fathers,
carrying baskets,
walked the banks of the Euphrates,
by the Hanging Gardens of Babylon
and the Garden of Eden,
in the Cradle of Civilization,
picking up pieces
of the bodies of their children,
pieces of their children,
pieces of their children.

The Kids from the Local Ashram

They come at weird hours,
Six thirty-six in the a.m.,
Two twenty-two in the afternoon,
The sunshine kids and their graying gurus,
Tripping up the walk,
Floating in the heat like space dancers,
Sticking their fingers in my doorbell.
"What the hell do you want, now? I shout.
"This is the One," they say.
And push him through the portal.
He stands there, in my doorway
Orchestrating a Himalayan smile
And faraway eyes.
"I hom de wan," he says.
"Yeah," I say. "Well, bless your bliss.
But I have peas to plant
And shit to shovel. Come out to the barn,
I'll let you meditate over the manure."
And for some strange reason they follow,
Talking about Cosmic consciousness
And Constant Karma.
Meanwhile, out in the barn,
Bumblebees buzz, thrums of bass fiddles,
Yellow-jackets swarm to sweat.
I hand them pitchforks.
"Spread it thin," I say. "No lumps."
Within ten minutes the enlightened ones
Are stumbling back down my drive,
Humming a Mantra and the Mosquito-bite Blues.

It's then I lean on my rake,
Watch them go and wonder why people
Who walk around with so much shit
Never learn to shovel.

The Treacherous Baker

Elliot,
you man of deceit,
you breaker of trusts,
how the hell can you bake bread
and treat your woman so?
Sly Elliot,
slyly convincing everyone to love you
and your damned bread.
And everyone loves you
except her, and me.
She used to love you,
I never did!
I did not know you when.
Were you like this before
you began baking bread,
or was it the killing of yeast
that drove you to it?
Elliot,
forty-four acres of whole wheat
and you use enriched flour.
I hope your efforts turn to mold.
I pray your ovens fail.
Elliot,
you are a small loaf.

Jim Killacky Criticizes One of My Poems

LeClaire, he says,
You're a bloody raver,
A manipulator.
You spew the words
As if you mean them,
As if you know what you say.
Catch yourself on,
It all comes to naught.
So why do you lie so, China?
My china plate,
My best, my mate?
You should have stuck
To writing about your women
Your whisky and your damn horses.
There's no cock-a-hoop
In that poem, lad.
You lost it;
You traded it away;
You spent it all
On bromidic, metaphysical shite.
Do you hear what I say, China?
You're a bloody cowboy
Talking through your bleeding hat.

Observations

"…for what we see is what we are."

~*Ernst Hass*

The River

The river
Is the sky
Is the river.

Trout rise,
Swim to the sun,
Swim back.

The face
Of a God
I had forgotten.

Image II

The river turns
back
Conclusion
comes
without reaching
An end

Image VI

sliver of sun
above the trees
three ducks coming in
short shadows,

fast, dark crosses
in the new, morning light

Boy with His Head on Fire

The sinking sun, burns the tops of redwoods
spiking up on the western hill.
In the corral the roan stands
head straight out like a fist on the end of an arm.
The red dog and the boy with his head on fire
watch.

On the Town Council's Ruling Not to Allow Farm Animals within City Limits

There are no chickens
in my grandfather's chicken coop,
no crowing cocks either,
just rolls of rusted barbed wire
and solidified bags of cement.
All at a time when we
so desperately need the eggs.

What We Know about Night

At first light, the cormorant
leaves the river,
without grace.

Wings beat the water to a froth,
it squawks loud, like a parrot, fucking in flight,
rises heavy as a cemetery,

flies west until
it's but a spot of midnight
and disappears over the horizon.

At dusk it returns,
from the east,
dragging night behind it.

Every Once and Unexpected

Driving back from Stanford
Mysterious, cold clouds roll in over the hills
From Half Moon Bay.
They're alive.
Every once and unexpected
One sighs, giving up a bit of breath,
A small geyser of vapor,
Carnelian over the green hills,
A sacrifice of sorts.
At an overpass I turn and head back
Towards that land of wealthy strangers
Where I left you
Until I find a turnout and stop.
Out of the car, I stand and watch the fog billow in,
Gray and blue and white and top-edged with red.
I piece together the pieces of the single piece.
An army of cars coming toward me slows to a crawl.
-What's he looking at?
-What does he see?
-There's nothing there!
I see what my life has taught me to see,
And understand there's a way of knowing
And why some of us witness what others pass by.
It has to do with still being amazed
By simple things,
Like this bit of found luck,
This bit of sea over the trees,
By the red-tail hawk diving into it,
Disappearing without a trace.
Wish you were here you'd be amazed.
                              - Love - Earl

April

"Even after all this time
The sun never says to the earth, "You owe me."
Look what happens with a Love like that!
—It lights the whole Sky."

~*Hafiz*

Prayer for a Husband

What are you waiting for
now that you know I am here?
If you wait, when you get here,
you will have seen me
and be in love with me,
but I'll be gone.
I'll have gone far away.
Perhaps, even,
to where you came from.

Distance

Me,
Fifty one,
stacking wood
like lines
in a poem.

You,
beneath the
plum tree,
stacking poems
like wood.

Me.
You.
And all
that distance
in between.

I Have Charted Now

I have charted, now
The coast of your body
And the depth of your grace
Made passage through your reef
Of bone and honey.

I have been becalmed
In the perfume of you
In the taste of you
In the stillness of you.

I woke to you and built a nest
On the island of your heart
Where I, now live
And drink from the spring
Of your eyes.

You, to whom I revealed
The harsh tract of my past
That burned blue-flame
In my bush of ghosts

That mad life of rage and sorrow
Left behind, now
In the ash of my ascension
Which was buoyed by your strength
And the fierceness of your kisses.

And here I give to you
And here I hold, for as long as you allow,
In the vault of your beauty,
In the open, white rose of your love.

Room Full of April

You enter a room
and the room fills with April.
Sunlight pours through the window,
water into a clay jar.
The floor becomes sand,
the walls, woven with bird wings,
fall away.
The air blossoms,
dogwood and lavender.
The roots of trees
whisper your name
in the stone soaked earth.

You enter a room
and a passageway,
carpeted with the grass
growing on the graves
of a thousand years, opens.
The world ascends
into itself and all
the myths that are you
stride down through the centuries.

This Morning

I listened

to the sounds
of water

as you drew
your bath.

Murmurings
of the river.

Rose petals raining
lightly on the lawn.

You, here.

The Mirror's Thin Edge

"I know now that there is no one thing that is true –
it is all true."

~Ernest Hemingway

Catching On

You go through lovers and friends
like the lonely through religions,
through wives
like the religious through saints.
And in the mornings,
when the alarm clock rings
like a phone you don't want to answer,
you spend time,
desperate and alone,
shaving the face of a foreigner
until you lose the image in the mirror's thin edge.

Catch yourself on,
you know what's out there,
you know what's within.

Yet you continue to lie,
like some unconvincing French existentialist,
telling yourself it's not caring
or caring too much,
that keeps you from either or both,
until you lose yourself
to an abstraction that becomes
the obliging nonsense of a lost self.

How many times have you told yourself,
"this is the last time,"
Knowing full well that the last time
is always the first,
and the first time never the last?

Catch yourself on.
It all comes to naught.
So why do you lie so?

You remember a woman you loved in Ruidoso,
and how, on the morning after the big race,
won by a long shot,
you woke to an empty room,
the winning ticket pilfered from your pocket.
You remember the name of a friend
and the newspaper clipping
with the details of his death,
sent to you by someone
who thought you would want to know.
You remember your first wife
and how it was;
your last wife,
and how it wasn't.
You remember, yet,
for all your remembering,
you cannot remember how to forget.
So, for you, time remains
in the mirror's thin edge.

Catch yourself on.
You know what's out there.
You know what's within.
These are no great secrets.
They never were.

Off The Isle of Shoals

"-sharks in the breakers...
again and again the ominous fin...
to swim is to dare."

Somewhere down the line
I stopped believing in gods,
in magic.
As in all the sound I hear,
only silence.
But there's a solace in this,
the knowing of a secret thing.
And I am finally old enough to say:
I want to spend time
with those who are connected
to the things of this earth
or else to be left alone.
If I was a drunk I'd be taller, braver.
But I'm only a poet
dancing on the graves of the living,
pissing on my own.
When I was young
I could take a heart
and fold it in the crease of a smile.
I'm sixty-three
hearts are not as pliable.
Some, in the happy crowd,
say I laugh too much,
talk too loud.
But I have been to the frontier,
spent time on the big two-hearted river
and that's farther,

I suppose, than most.
So I don't expect
understanding.
Even from those
whom I believe would understand.
And I accept what I find
and, I tell you,
it's better than all holy and voodoo.
When I was a boy
I'd walk behind old man Panciera's plow
looking for arrowheads.
When I found them
I'd squeeze them
until they drew blood again.
Until I felt the hand
that shaped it.
Now the farms are owned by Purina.
The land posted.
Man
no longer sees
the connection
between the sky and the tree,
the tree and the horse,
the horse and the sea,
the sea and earth,
earth and man.
I have had breakfasts
of raw clams and beach plums.
Seen the green flash,
have lain in oceans
of golden meadows
and let insects crawl over me,
my thoughts of nothing.

This morning,
I am alone in a sixteen foot boat
off the isle of shoals.
On a nearby island,
the faithful are repairing the roof
of an ancient, stone church,
and singing hymns to Jesus.
The name floats down
like a shot goose,
settles on the water,
close,
sinks without a trace.
Farther out,
three shapes rise,
tread water,
disappear.
I consider them.
But, it's morning.
the sun fills the east
like a flute of champagne
and the sea is so still
that the dead,
who pull the bell ropes
of the buoys and nuns,
are still asleep
in the deep, wet catacombs
beneath.
I listen carefully.
And, again,
in all the sound I hear,
only silence.
So I get out this pen,
this paper,
and begin this poem to you.

Prayer for the Living and the Dead

I am your witness:
through the bones of winter,
through the hospitals of survival,
through the surrenders of safe harbors,
through the funerals of April,
through the ruins of memories,
through the myths of genetics,
through the lust of lies,
through the locust of doubt,
through the famines of love,
through the religions of loneliness,
to the roots of your loss.

Your mother killed herself.
It was not your fault, or mine,
nor was it hers.
It was dead dragons on the doorstep,
the holy and voodoo in the mirror of history;
the unknown in the equation of circumstance.

So let us, now,
the living and the dead,
lean into each other, make room,
and enter the unbound chambers
of the heart.

The Ride Out

You ride the commuter bus from Boulder,
east, up the slip-grade at Table Mesa,
to meet the sun released hours ago
by friends in Delaware.
On the plateau, between housing compounds,
horses graze, Spanish, on short grass.
And in the silver light
you imagine this land to be Arapahoe.
Sawtoothed lodges appear at the brim of a bright river.
Bison. Antelope. Eagle. Elk.

But the road bends south,
the sun wanes, sour wheat,
and nothing you can name
will hold this image against the day,
against the sounds of Boulevard and Broadway,
against small rooms in which crowds of people
ascend, like sullen miners, to yet other rooms.

If you had been born to buckskin
and your name, Colter,
the South Platte would still flow from the foothills
through cottonwood and chokecherry.
But your name is Edward,
the day is diesel,
and you will spend it
trying to remember the scent of a distant snow
while imaginary buffalo grass swirls
around your feet
and a fossil sea echoes
home
in the lost shell of your ear.

Knuckleheads

"We are trying to save the world,
one knucklehead at a time."

~Allen "Chris" Christenbury, Cove Creek Farm

There is a face in the clock,
not of the clock
but in the clock,
a reminder that we each have
one journey, one time through,
only one chance to get it right.

And yet, heedless, young men,
stand alone in the shadows,
through twenty-four hour midnights,
exposed, with no armistice
or clear morning in sight,
searching for something they
have forgotten the name of,
terrorizing themselves and others with
bayonet posturing and knife-edge lies.
These, the self-deceived,
have become the men
we've tried to keep them from.

These, our sons, our brothers,
amiss with million dollar dreams
and a nickel's worth of understanding,
hide in the basements
of their Paleolithic brains,
shuffle aimlessly through the stark
and barren landscapes of their minds,

while cannibalistic parasites
of drugs and self-deception,
mistaken for armor
against the world,
against bad memories,
against that fear of other,
feed on them like a cancer until
they are permanently maimed or dead.

Death is easy.
Fear is the tenant of the weak;
that dread of life that never allows you
to accept what is,
that never allows you
to understand
that you don't have anything to prove.

Stay then, where darkness is the dictator
and let the earth receive you
without prayer, without parade,
without mourning as the last light
of your flesh is covered with the gasping scent
of decaying carnations and you disappear.

Or find the courage to return
to the promise of your lives.
Dare to look into that abyss
and pick through the shards and rubble
for whatever it is that you can find
that is beauty,
for that one thing that is true.
Brave the art of living:
how to do for others,

how to let others do for you;
master the art of healing,
learn the art of love.
The world has been bloodied more than enough
with the rust and ruins of lives lived badly.

Poacher

Norman,
That year you crouched on your tree-stand,
above the Cumberland Monastery,
I killed nine deer.
Not one got twenty yards
before the blood pumped out
giving up the life.

I made money.

All but one sold to game clubs
in New York City.

I got good.

I killed 122 wood duck
in a single day's shoot:
leading them five at a time in my eye of eyes,
the Winchester Fifty, plug out,
five shots,
five birds falling
before the gun's rolling thunder stopped echoing
across the cornfield;
the gun-barrel smoking
from the heat of it.
Enough lead shot through it
to build a ship's anchor.

I made money.

I got a buck apiece for the ducks,
two for the feathered skins.
Bucktail. Squirrel tail. Neck-
hackle and coverts from upland game birds.
Sold to fly-tiers and haberdashers.

I got good.

I killed a black bear and a pig gone feral
up by my sister's place.
Canadian geese. American Brant.
Woodcock. Green-winged Teal.
Puddle jumpers. Divers.

And not all with a gun.
Some with cunning, deception,
sheer villainy.
I staked #8 chicken wire
a foot below the surface of the pond,
six inches to bottom,
spread corn, left it for geese.
In the morning they'd be there:
drowned heads of cabbage
ready for the cutting.
I collected pea-brain birds,
pheasant, quail,
too dumb to exit a spiraling maze.
Wrung their necks.
Filled the game bags.
In the evenings I sat beneath overhanging pine
with a scoped .22,
waiting for ruffled grouse, the partridge,
to roost in the bare limbs

of ironwood and stripped laurel.
I'd slip a rubber nipple over the muzzle,
sight in on a silhouette,
aim for the head,
and PPPSSTTT!!!, before the gas could bang.
I'd get six or seven this way
before they'd catch on.

And on and on it went:
from October to Christmas.
Enough blood to make a butcher blush.
Then it stopped, for reasons
I still find hard to explain.
But I'll try.

Picture this:
the shotgun, empty, chamber open,
resting across a rotting stump,
pointing North,
like the needle of a good compass.
Me, huddling a small fire,
chewing the half-cooked liver
of the last deer.
The wind kicks up,
blows down the gun-barrel
like breath down a hollow bone.
The gun issues a low moan,
a wail, almost,
and for a second, not much more,
I hear the roots of trees
whisper my name
in the death-soaked earth.

Night Taxi

The bartenders have all gone home
and it's just me and the tweekers
and Sheriff, One Lincoln Eleven
down on channel nine.
The moon is high and alone
like a cue-ball on a table that's been run.
And I can't help but wonder
what I'm doing here,
a cabbie, on the night shift,
in Pomo, sitting
in the American lotus position, waiting
for the cell phone to wink green.
When I face the rearview mirror squarely,
I am no longer thirty-three.
I am fifty-four.
Wrists gone, waist gone, my green age gone,
pissed away as quick as a green impulse
down an optic fiber.
I'm an aging lion
limping across the pampas
sitting, now, under the lights at Safeway,
staring out over the pavement.
I could drive up to Ranchero Heights.
I know the gate code.
When they lock behind me I would be secure.
and drive to the top of the hill,
and rich and closer to the moon.
But inside me there's an old trail
like the summer memory of an icy comet;
a path that leads from a place I call,
the Badlands.

I need to get beyond it;
back to I-Death,
back to the headwaters
of the Big Two-Hearted River
where native brook trout,
spotted with new year's confetti
and sides as slick as gun barrels,
hide under green, moss grown banks
and hold against the current.
Back to the streams where big German browns
sulk at the bottoms of quiet pools.
To Weekapaug, Misquamicut
and Block Island Sound
where striped bass and bluefish break
as far as the eye can see.
I need to recite the names
of the places I loved best:
PerryHealy, MeadowBrook, Quonotataug,
The Great Swamp, Watchaug,
Moonstone Beach, Deckers,
and Cheeseman Canyon,
Schoolhouse Pond, Napatree Point,
Weekapaug, Chibugamoo
Saint James Bay, Sugar Grove,
over and over and over
like the mantra of the bell buoys
off the Isles of Shoals
and Watch Hill Reef.
Over and over until all the past is finally,
just the past, and my ghosts
are no longer allowed to live in my house.
Over and over until I hammer out a new plan
to carry me out of the Badlands on my way
towards morning, and homeward bound.

Earl In Upheaval

When I lost sixty-seven pounds
and bought that L.L. Bean uniform:
forest-green shirt, tan slacks, barn coat
and Birkenstock clogs
the color of creamed coffee,
one mother-of-pearl stud earring,
I made a real commitment to the new me.

I purchased a Volvo
with matching air-bags.
A white, leather couch,
companion loveseat and a genuine
Persian rug to put them on.
Found a classic Beamer.
I got my teeth fixed, implants,
Top of the line.
Joined the Hair Club for Men,
partial treatment.
I pulled down the Dave Best painting,
the one with the Madonna, Christ and skulls.
Put up travel posters:
An English Countryside;
A German castle;
A Safe Harbor in Spain.
I moved my son and his music into the garage,
built him his own bathroom.
Gave away the Coltrane,
the Monk, the Mingus Among Us,
the John Zorn
and the Elliot Sharp
LP's and CD's.

I burned the Social Dogs.
Took up with Inya and Kitaro,
Sounds of the Seashore.
I banished the blue healer to a pen in the yard.
Brought home a toy schnauzer,
registered,
Best of Breed.
I changed my diet:
gave-up day-old coffee
for herbal teas,
cleared the refrigerator of all meats,
eighty-sixed the Stilton Blue and the Brie,
the Half and Half,
replaced them with Rella and Rice Dream,
stocked in strange vegetables: arugula, jicima,
mesclun salad mix, baby bok choy.
I sold off the unfiltered Coturi Zin,
laid in a supply of Evian,
Perrier,
Mendocino.
Got rid of the guns:
the over & under Winchester .12 gauge,
the 9 mm Sig Sauer P250,
fourteen in the clip, one in the chamber,
the sweet, smooth shoulder holster,
the ammunition, the gun oil.
I signed up for Aikido,
bowed to O Sensei two hours a week.
I threw away the race results and the morning line,
And took to reading The New York Times,
The Wall Street Journal,
Dow/Jones Averages, NASDAQ.
Had a cellular phone installed in the BMW.

Took speech lessons.
Studied a foreign language,
my diction elegant,
my pronunciation perfect,
my vocabulary laced with menu French:
paté, château briand, vichyssoise,
and beyond: Les Miserable,
eau d'toilet.

I joined the Wheel People.
Peugeot 21 speed,
snappy helmet,
Spandex.

I went to a channeler:
got in touch with my past life,
Ming Po. Chinese Emperor.
Benevolent Ruler Absolute!
(Of course I expected nothing less).
Went to a holistic healer:
Bach Flowers.
ball-bearings in my ears,
massage and understanding,
enzyme baths,
therapy to touch the child within,
became childish but not child-like.

I organized a men's sensitivity group.
Gave up profanity.
Learned to cry.
Listened sympathetically to my wife and women,
empathized,
Venery became a thing of the past.

I began to smile a lot.
I began to
            float.

Then it all came crashing down.
Not all at once,
It took at least a day and a half.
It began with the well-dressed woman
standing in line at the East-West Cafe
waiting for her double, double decaff latte,
with cinnamon and dark Swiss chocolate,
complaining about the quality of her life.
Certainly it had something to do
with Darfur, 9-11, Iraq,
the boy in the bubble.
the Washington and Wall Street Punks
in their pin-striped suits
and power ties, hands in the till,
the homeless around me,
and more.
I reverted.

I reverted back
to black t-shirts
emblazoned with skulls,
roses in their teeth,
cut-off jeans, and sandals.
I chucked the earring,
apologized to my son,
and wrestled him to a draw
while playing Zappa, Reggae,
and Bartok, all at the same time,

FULL VOLUME.
I let the healer back inside,
and the last we saw of the schnauzer
was it's ass at the end of my foot.
I bought a box of hand rolled Havanas,
pre-embargo, -chain smoked them,
shot skeet off the back porch,
buck-naked and swearing,
scared the B-Jesus out of the realtor
and the prospective buyers for the house next door.
I tracked mud across the living room floor,
pissed outside,
spent a night with my wife
on a sand bar
in the middle of the Russian River
under the twelve moons of Jupiter
we located Andromeda.
I swilled dago-red by the bucket-full,
wrote long, involved letters
to friends in prison and insane asylums,
and to those less fortunate
living in gated communities.
I reread Robert Stone. Leslie Silko. Cormac
McCarthy. John Hawks. Malcom Lowery.
Dennis Johnson. **Muriel** Rukeyser. Bukowski.
Ruth Weiss. Bob Kaufman. Lucas Shepard.
Balzac. Russell Hoban. Denise Mina.
Yeats. Shelley and Keats. Neruda.
I studied Richard Hugo's,
"What thou Lovest Well Remains American."
Wallace Stevens', "Notes Toward A Supreme Fiction".
Brady T. Brady's,
"Making Things Work", and "One Man's Meat".

Reconsidered the Chaos Theory
and fractal equations.
I put art back up on the walls.
My wife's prints in the living room,
the kitchen, the studio, the hall.
Denny Moer's photographs,
and those of the Shackleton Expedition,
a pastel by Stacia Limon,
an assemblage by Best,
photographs of all the kids.
I brought the Karma Sutra oils, body paints,
and Sal Guardino's erotic etchings
back into the bedroom.
I wrecked the Beamer,
totaled the Volvo.
Invited half a million people over for a cookout.
We grilled venison steaks,
roasted raccoon,
rabbit, opossum, squirrel,
road-kill,
no more than a few hours old,
smothered them with onions
and barbeque sauce.
I danced like a Gypsy,
howled like a lunatic,
gave thanks to Whatever and All
because Mary, Joseph and Hallelujah,
it sure was a close one.

The Art of Letters

E-mail has reinvented the art of letters,
brought unexpected connections,
renewed acquaintances, some
puzzling, most welcomed.

"The season has been
hectic," she writes.
"…I want the simplicity
of a monk's life, (like yours?),

no one around, no holidays,
no religion, no news,
no kids, no people,
no poetry, no nothing,

except perhaps a river
quietly flowing, but with a switch
to shut off the sound.
I will write again in a week or so."

I write back but
it's the things I leave out.
I don't tell her

that I spent the holidays
odd man out, because
I have not taken Jesus
as my Personal Savior,

do not drive with a bumper sticker
that reads: My Child Is An Honor Student,
do not own a Disney
sweat shirt, t-shirt, pencil, pen or mug,

that I have become an information
junkie, addicted to the World Wide Web,
that my son is in Iraq with the 25th Infantry,
that on occasion I still attempt to write poems,

that the river I live beside,
swollen with winter rain and snow melt,
is raging, the sound deafening.
I also leave out the fact

that I am like Mr. Merriweather
in Little Big Man, who,
every time Jack Crabb sees him,
is missing another part,

that I now have one good leg
and a bad back,
that my teeth, finished off
by a second lightning strike,

are replaced with a plate and a partial,
that I no longer need to shave my head,
and the fierce, bald look
I carried before isn't what it use to be,

more Buddha now, both, head and belly,
that they took out my thyroid,
that the muscles have melted to fat,
that I suffer gonadal droop, balls twisting

in my underwear, dropping into toilet water,
that memory would be non existent
without Ginko and a bevy
of supplements and meds every morning,

that I can't read without lenses,
can't hear without an ear amp in place,
that I might as well be a monk
for all the good my pecker does me,

and that, in spite of it all,
I am doing well or at least
as well as can be expected.
I can't wait for her next e-mail.

Jonquils

Everything I remember crowds me
                       Memory is a black hole
                    collapsing
an
               implosion
Memories' matter
crushed into a form   so dense
        it prevents
seeing
     new

Try to shine a light on memory
                    and the light
disappears into it
No il-
lumination   So I try
not to remember,
to forget
everything
so everything is
       new
The jonquils are in bloom   I refuse to remem-
ber
what
they smell like
so
                 I go
out
They smell like nothing I have ever smelled before,
so fragrant   and sweet
a clarifying

light
I cannot remem-
ber
the ocean   So seeing it
again,
beneath
an endless blue
vault,
breaking against the rocks
foamy and white-green like glass   A clarifying
light
A new sunrise
in my eyes   new

                                                  new

il-
luminating,   new
radiating out
                         in   ever expanding
circles
                 New